The Elves and the Shoemaker
The Magpie's Nest
Thomas and the Toad
The Farmer and the Donkey
The King's Lazy Soldiers
The Strawberry Boy
The Magic Kettle
Foolish Jack
The Three Wishes

CONTENTS

this book belongs to Melany parker

British Library Cataloguing in Publication Data
Randall, Ronne P
Goodnight stories.
I. Title II. Russell, Chris
813'.54[J] PZ7
ISBN 0-7214-7538-8

First edition

Published by Ladybird Books Ltd Loughborough Leicestershire UK
Ladybird Books Inc Auburn Maine 04210 USA

Printed in England

Goodnight Stories

compiled by Ronne P Randall
illustrated by Chris Russell

Ladybird Books

The twelve dancing princesses

Once there was a king who had twelve beautiful daughters. They all slept in the same room, and when they went to bed each night, the king locked and bolted their door. But every morning when he opened the door, he found that their shoes were completely worn through.

'How can this be?' the king wondered. 'What do my daughters do each night?'

At last the king announced that anyone who could find out how his daughters wore out their shoes could choose one of the princesses to be his wife.

The next day a prince came to try his luck. He was taken to a room next to the princesses' bedroom, and was told to keep watch. So that he could see what the princesses did, the door to their room was left open.

Before long the prince's eyelids grew heavy. He tried hard to stay awake, but he couldn't. When he woke up the next morning, the princesses' shoes were again worn through. The prince had failed, and he had to leave the palace.

Many more young men came and tried their luck, but none succeeded.

One day a poor soldier decided to try and learn the princesses' secret. On his way to the palace, he met an old woman. 'I can help you,' she said. 'If you want to find out where the princesses go and what they do, don't drink anything they bring you. Just pretend to fall fast asleep.' Then she gave him a cloak. 'When you put this on, you will be invisible,' she said. 'You'll be able to follow the princesses wherever they go!'

So the soldier made his way to the palace. Like the others before him, he was taken to a room next to the princesses'. Before long, the eldest princess came in and gave him a goblet of wine.

Remembering what the old woman had told him, the soldier only pretended to drink the wine. Then he lay down, and after a little while he began to snore as if he were asleep.

When the princesses heard him, they got up and dressed in their finest clothes and jewels. They scurried about happily, preening and primping and putting ribbons in their hair. When they were ready, they looked at the soldier again. He was still snoring. 'We are safe,' whispered the eldest princess.

The eldest princess then went to her bed and tapped on it. It sank into the floor and became a wide staircase. One by one, all the princesses went down the stairs.

The soldier, who had seen everything, didn't waste a minute. He threw the magic cloak over his shoulders and followed the princesses down the staircase.

At the bottom of the stairs, there was a row of splendid trees. The leaves were silver, and they sparkled and glittered. 'I'd better take something to prove where I've been,' thought the soldier. He broke off one of the branches and hid it under his cloak.

Next they came to a row of trees with leaves of gold. Once again the soldier thought, 'I'd better take something back with me,' and he broke off a golden branch.

Finally they came to a row of trees with leaves of pure shimmering diamonds. The soldier took one of these branches, too.

On they went, until they came to a wide river. Twelve boats were waiting at the bank, with a handsome prince in each one. Each prince helped a princess into his boat. The soldier got into the last boat, with the youngest princess. 'I don't know why,' said her prince, 'but the boat seems very heavy tonight. I have to row with all my strength just to make it move!'

On the other side of the river there was a magnificent palace. It was ablaze with lights, and lively music came from within. The princes rowed across the river and everyone went inside.

There, in a vast ballroom, each prince danced with his princess, whirling and twirling

to the music of trumpets and drums. They danced and danced, until three in the morning. By then all the princesses' shoes were worn through, and they had to stop.

The princes rowed them back across the river, and this time the soldier sat in the first boat, with the eldest princess. On the bank, the princesses said goodbye to their princes, and promised to come again the following night.

When they reached the staircase, the soldier ran on ahead. He quickly climbed into his bed, hiding the three branches under his pillow. By the time the princesses came in, his eyes were closed and he was snoring loudly once again. 'No need to worry about him,' said the eldest princess.

The princesses put away their fine clothes and jewels. Then they put their worn out shoes under their beds and went to sleep.

The next morning the soldier went to the king.

'Now,' said the king, 'can you tell me what my daughters have been doing every night?'

'Yes,' replied the soldier. 'They have been dancing with twelve princes in an underground palace.' He told the king everything that had happened, and showed him the three branches.

The king sent for his daughters and asked them whether the soldier was telling the truth. Though they were sorry that their secret had been discovered, they knew that they could not lie. 'Yes,' they said. 'It is true.'

So the king asked the soldier which princess he wanted to marry. The soldier chose the eldest, and they lived happily ever after. But the twelve princesses never again went dancing in the magnificent underground palace.

The three sillies

There was once a girl named Margaret who had a sweetheart named Henry. One evening Margaret's mother and father invited Henry to stay for supper, and they sent Margaret down to the cellar for a jug of cider.

While she was down there, Margaret happened to look up at the ceiling. There, stuck in one of the beams, was a great big hammer.

'Goodness me, that looks dangerous!' thought Margaret. 'What if Henry and I get married, and we have a son, and he grows up, and we send him down to the cellar for cider, and the hammer falls down and hits him on the head? What a dreadful thing that would be!' She was so upset that she dropped the jug of cider and began to cry.

Upstairs, everyone was wondering what was taking Margaret so long. 'I'd better go down and look for her,' said her mother.

She found Margaret sitting crying, with the jug broken and the cider running all over the floor. 'Why, Margaret, whatever is the matter?' she asked.

'Oh, Mother,' cried Margaret, 'look at that awful hammer up there! What if Henry and I get married and have a son, and he grows up and comes down to the cellar for cider, and the hammer falls down and hits him on the head? What a dreadful thing that would be!'

'Oh, you're right!' said her mother. 'That *would* be dreadful!' And she sat down beside Margaret and started crying, too.

After a while, Margaret's father began to wonder why his wife and daughter hadn't come back, and he went down to the cellar to look for them. There the two sat crying, with the cider running all over the floor. 'Whatever is the matter?' he asked.

'Just look at that awful hammer!' said his wife. 'Imagine what would happen if our daughter and Henry got married, and they had a son, and he grew up and came down to the cellar for cider, and the hammer fell down and hit him on the head. Wouldn't that be dreadful?'

'Dear, oh dear,' said her husband. 'That *would* be dreadful!' And he sat down beside them and started crying, too.

At last Henry got tired of sitting in the kitchen by himself, and he went down to the cellar to see what had happened to everyone. There the three sat crying, side by side, with the cider running all over the floor.

'What on earth is wrong?' Henry asked.

'Look at that awful hammer!' said Margaret's father. 'What if you and Margaret get married, and you have a son, and he grows up and comes down to the cellar for cider, and the hammer falls down and hits him on the head?' And all three started crying even harder than before.

Henry just burst out laughing, and reached up and pulled out the hammer. 'I've travelled many miles,' he said, 'but I've never met such three big sillies as you. Soon I'll be off on my travels again. When I find three bigger sillies than you, I'll come back and marry Margaret.'

Henry set out the very next day. After travelling a long way, he came to a cottage that had grass growing on the roof. A woman was standing outside the cottage, trying to get a cow to climb up a ladder. The animal wouldn't move.

'What are you doing?' Henry asked the woman.

'Why, look at all that nice grass growing up there,' she replied. 'I'm trying to get the cow onto the roof so that she can eat it.'

'Oh, you poor silly!' said Henry. 'Why don't you just cut the grass and throw it down to the cow?'

'I never thought of that!' said the woman. 'Thank you!'

As he went on his way, Henry thought, 'Well, that was one big silly!'

Henry went on and on, and at last he stopped at an inn for the night. The inn was so crowded that the landlord had to put Henry in a room with another traveller.

The next morning, when they were both getting up, Henry was amazed to see the other man hang his trousers on the chest of drawers, and then run across the room and try to jump into them. He tried over and over again, but he just couldn't do it. At last he stopped to catch his breath.

'Oh me, oh my,' he puffed, mopping his brow with a handkerchief. 'I think trousers are the most difficult clothes ever invented. It takes me hours to get into mine, and I get so tired! How do you manage yours?'

Henry burst out laughing, and showed the man how to put on his trousers. The man was very grateful. 'I never would have thought of doing it that way myself!' he said.

'Well, that's another big silly,' thought Henry.

Henry set out on his travels again, and that evening he came to a pond near a village. A crowd of people stood around the pond, and they were all reaching into it with rakes and brooms and shovels.

'What are you doing?' asked Henry.

'Can't you see?' they cried. 'The moon's tumbled into the pond, and we're trying to get it out again!'

Henry burst out laughing, and told them to look up in the sky. 'The moon's still there,' he said. 'That's just its reflection in the water!'

But the people became very angry and wouldn't listen to him. 'If you won't help us, you'd better leave,' they said.

'Well,' thought Henry, going on his way. 'There's a whole crowd of sillies bigger than the three sillies at home!'

So Henry went back home and married Margaret, and he never called her or her parents silly again.

Thomas and the toad

There was once a king who had three sons. The two older sons were outspoken and clever, but the youngest son, Thomas, hardly ever said a word, so everyone thought he was a fool.

One day the king thought, 'It's time I decided which of my sons will become king after me.' He called his sons together and said, 'Go out and search, and whichever one of you brings me the finest carpet will have my crown and my kingdom.'

To make sure his sons didn't all go off in the same direction, the king took them outside and blew three feathers into the air. 'Go as they fly,' he said.

One feather flew east, and that was where the eldest son was to go. The second feather flew west, and that was where the middle son was to go. But the third feather just fell to the ground. 'Poor little Thomas!' his brothers laughed as they rode off. 'He doesn't have the chance to go anywhere!'

Thomas sat down feeling very sad. Then he caught sight of a strange-looking rock on the ground, not far from the feather. There was a door in the rock, and Thomas opened it. Inside there was a ladder. He climbed down the ladder, and at the bottom he found a big fat toad, surrounded by ten little frogs. 'What can I do for you?' the toad asked Thomas.

'I'm looking for the finest carpet in the world,' Thomas replied.

The toad turned to one of the little frogs. 'Bring me my box,' she said.

The little frog came back with a big wooden box, and the toad opened it. Inside was a carpet so fine and beautiful that it could not have been woven by human hands. The toad gave the carpet to Thomas, who thanked her, and went back up the ladder.

Meanwhile, the two elder brothers thought Thomas was still at home. 'He'll never find a beautiful carpet,' they said, 'so we don't even have to bother looking for one.' Instead, they got a shawl from the first peasant woman they met, and brought that back to their father.

The king was disappointed. 'I expected something a little finer than this,' he told his sons. Then Thomas arrived. When the king saw how beautiful his carpet was, he was delighted. 'You shall have my kingdom, Thomas,' he said.

The two older sons were furious. 'It isn't right,' they told their father. 'Thomas is a fool. How can you give the kingdom to him?'

'All right,' said the king, at last. 'I will give you another task. This time, the one who brings me the most beautiful ring will have my kingdom.'

Again the king took his sons outside, blew three feathers into the air, and told his sons to follow the feathers. Again the first two feathers went east and west. But Thomas's feather just fell to the ground, next to the rock with the door in it.

'Perhaps that toad will help me again,' Thomas thought, and he opened the door and went down the ladder.

'What do you want now?' asked the toad when she saw Thomas.

'The most beautiful ring in the world,' Thomas replied.

The toad called for her wooden box, and took out a gold ring set with glittering gems. It was so beautiful that no jeweller on earth could have made it. The toad gave the ring to Thomas, who quickly took it back to his father's castle.

Thomas's brothers thought Thomas was too stupid to know what a beautiful ring looked like, much less where to find one. So they didn't bother looking for one themselves. They just pulled some nails out of a fence post and brought them to their father.

'These aren't very beautiful,' said the king. Then Thomas arrived with his ring. 'Now *this* is a ring fit for a king!' said his father. 'The kingdom is yours, Thomas.'

But once again the two elder brothers pestered their father, until at last he agreed to give them one more task. The kingdom, he said, would go to the son who brought back the most beautiful maiden. Again he blew three feathers into the air, and again they fell as they had before.

Thomas went straight to the fat toad and said, 'I need to find the most beautiful maiden in the world.'

'Oh, really?' said the toad. 'She isn't here just now, but you can have one of my little frogs instead.'

'What good will a frog be to me?' asked Thomas.

'If you don't want her, I can't help you,' said the toad, and she began to hop away.

'All right,' said Thomas. 'I suppose a frog is better than nothing.'

The toad gave him a hollowed-out potato with six mice harnessed to it. 'Choose one of my little frogs and put her inside,' she said.

Thomas chose the smallest frog and put her in the potato. As soon as she was in it, the frog turned into the loveliest maiden Thomas had ever seen. The potato turned into a splendid carriage, and the six mice turned into horses.

Thomas jumped into the carriage, kissed the maiden, and drove straight to his father's castle. 'She is indeed beautiful,' said the king, when Thomas brought the maiden to him.

Then Thomas's brothers arrived. They hadn't bothered to look for beautiful maidens, but had brought two servant girls from their father's own kitchen. When the king saw them he said, 'My kingdom will go to Thomas – and that is my *final* decision!'

The brothers knew that there was nothing more they could do. Thomas became king, married the beautiful maiden, and together the two reigned wisely and happily for many long years.

Mog and Mag and the bucket

Many years ago an old man named Mog lived with his wife, Mag, in a little cottage in the country. Because it was a very old cottage, it didn't have a sink, and the dishes had to be washed in a big bucket. Each evening, after all the dishes had been washed, Mag would put the day's vegetable peelings – all the potato skins and onion skins and carrot scrapings – into the bucket of dirty water. Then Mog would take the bucket outside and empty it over the garden wall.

In the morning the neighbour's pig would come by and snuffle up any vegetable peelings that hadn't soaked through the ground. He thought they were delicious, and

Mog and Mag liked to see him enjoying himself.

One evening, just as the moon was rising, Mog went out to empty the bucket as usual. He was just about to pour the dirty water and vegetable peelings over the garden wall, when he saw someone watching him. It was a tiny little man, someone Mog had never seen before. The stranger was dressed in an odd, old fashioned suit, and he had enormous brown shoes on his feet.

'Oh, dear,' said the strange little man, pointing to the bucket. 'I do wish you wouldn't do that!'

'But I've emptied this bucket here every evening for thirty years,' said Mog.

'Yes, I know,' sighed the stranger. 'That's what's been upsetting me.'

'Upsetting you?' exclaimed Mog. 'What does this bucket have to do with you?'

'Well, perhaps I can show you,' said the stranger. 'Come and stand on my shoes.'

'Stand on your shoes?' cried Mog. He had never met anyone so peculiar!

'Yes,' said the little man. 'That's the only way I can show you my home.'

'Well, all right,' said Mog, not wanting to be impolite. He went and put his feet on the stranger's big shoes.

As he did so, something astonishing happened. The ground turned clear as glass, and Mog could see right through it. Just beneath the spot where he and the little man were standing, there was a cottage very much like his own. Only this cottage was covered with muck! Dirty dishwater dripped down the walls. There were potato peelings all over the roof, carrot scrapings stuck to the windows, and onion skins clogging the drainpipe.

'Dear me!' gasped Mog. 'What a mess!'

'Yes,' said the little man, 'and it's even worse inside. The dirty water comes right through the chimney and splashes all over everything. There are potato skins in my bed and carrot scrapings in my saucepans. No matter how hard I try, I can't keep anything clean. You can imagine what it's like, after thirty years!'

'That *is* terrible,' said Mog. 'I do want to help you, but I'm not sure how. After all, my wife depends on me to empty that bucket for her. And what would the neighbour's pig do without his breakfast?'

'Oh, please,' begged the little man, 'please try to think of something. I don't think I can stand it much longer!' His eyes filled with tears.

Mog's heart ached for the little stranger. 'Don't worry,' he said. 'I'll have a talk with my wife, and I'm sure we'll be able to think of something. Don't you worry!'

'Thank you,' said the stranger, drying his eyes. 'Thank you!'

Then Mog stepped off the little man's shoes, and, without another word, the stranger vanished.

Mog went inside and told his wife what had happened. Mag just sat and listened, shaking her head from time to time. When Mog had finished, she gave a great sigh.

'The poor man,' she said. 'We have to do something to help him – but what?'

'I don't know,' said Mog. 'We'll have to think hard.'

So Mog and Mag sat by the fire and thought and thought. They sat and thought all night, and by the time the sun rose they had a plan.

Later that morning, a builder and a carpenter came to Mog and Mag's cottage. The builder took the door off its hinges, blocked up the doorway, and made a new opening at the back of the cottage. The carpenter made a sturdy new door to fit the opening, and he hung it on shiny new hinges.

That evening, when Mog went out of the door to empty the bucket, he went out to the *back* of the cottage, far from the garden wall. Now any dirty water and vegetable peelings that soaked through the ground would fall far away from the little man's cottage below. And the neighbour's pig could still come by for his breakfast in the morning.

Mog never saw the strange little man again. But every Saturday night from then on, he and Mag found a shiny penny under their new door. Now who do you suppose could have left it there?

The strawberry boy

Once upon a time, there was a couple who had no children. Every day they wished for a child, even a tiny one no bigger than a berry. At last their wish came true, and they had a little boy just the size of a strawberry.

The man and woman loved their son dearly and cared for him tenderly, but he never grew an inch. Still, he was a clever child, and he became more and more clever as he grew older.

One day, when the strawberry boy was sixteen years old, he was sitting in an eggshell on the kitchen table, keeping his mother company as she worked. His mother turned to him and said, 'You are growing up now. What do you want to be when you are a man?'

'I would like to be a messenger,' said the strawberry boy.

His mother burst out laughing. 'What an idea!' she said. 'With your tiny legs, it would take you an hour to go as far as most people go in a minute!'

But the strawberry boy said, 'I know I can do it, Mother. Just send me on an errand and see how fast I get back.'

'All right,' said his mother. 'Go to your aunt in the next village and get me a thimble.'

The strawberry boy jumped off the table and ran into the street. There he found a man on horseback who was just leaving for the next village. He climbed up the horse's leg, sat down under the saddle, and began to pinch the horse's side. The horse lunged and reared and began galloping with all its might, and nothing its rider did could slow it down.

When they reached the next village, the strawberry boy stopped pinching the horse, and the poor tired creature slowed down at last. As they passed his aunt's house, the strawberry boy slid down the horse's leg and ran inside. He got the thimble his mother wanted, then returned home the same way he had come.

His mother was amazed when he handed her the thimble. 'How did you get back so quickly?' she asked.

'Never mind, Mother,' the boy replied. 'But you see now that I was right, don't you? I can do anything I want to do!'

One evening, a few weeks later, the strawberry boy said to his parents, 'I am going out into the world to make my fortune. I'll come back when I'm rich.'

His parents laughed. 'How can someone as tiny as you get rich?' they said. 'You'd better stay here with us, where you're safe.'

'No,' said the strawberry boy. 'I *will* get rich, you'll see. I can do anything I want to do!'

His parents didn't believe him, but they kissed him goodbye and wished him luck anyway.

The strawberry boy climbed up onto the roof, where some storks had been nesting all summer. He crept onto the back of the biggest stork and tied himself to its wing with a silk thread. Then he snuggled into its soft feathers and went to sleep.

Winter was coming, and the next morning the storks set off on their long journey south. The strawberry boy flew through the air, safe on his stork's back. After many days they reached the warm sunny land where the storks spent the winter.

When the people of this land saw the strawberry boy, they were amazed, and they took him and his stork to their king. The king was delighted with the tiny fellow, and he put him in a special little box that he kept next to his throne. Soon he grew so fond of the boy that he gave him a huge diamond as a present. The strawberry boy fastened the diamond securely around his stork's neck with a ribbon.

In a few months, the storks were ready to make the journey back north. The strawberry boy climbed onto his stork's back, and away they went.

After travelling for a long time, the strawberry boy finally arrived back at his own home. He ran inside to fetch his parents.

'I told you I'd come back rich!' he said. 'Look what I've brought you!' He untied the ribbon from the stork's neck, and the diamond fell to the ground.

His parents knew then that their wonderful strawberry boy could indeed do anything he wanted to do. They all settled down to live happily, and the clever strawberry boy kept them rich for the rest of their lives.

The Sun and the fish

One evening, just as he was setting in the west, the Sun slipped and fell SPLASH! into the sea. The whole world became dark, and the Moon had to come out early to shine in the Sun's place.

The Moon was *very* angry. 'That Sun gets more and more careless every day,' she said. 'And just look at him now – blowing bubbles as if it didn't matter! Well, I can't put him back again. He's too heavy. The sailors will have to think of a way to do it.'

'We already have,' said the sailors. 'We're going to pull the Sun out of the water, as if we were pulling up an anchor. All we need is a strong rope.'

They searched everywhere, and at last they found just the right rope. It was as thick as a tree trunk, and so heavy that it took hundreds of sailors just to pick it up.

They tied one end of the huge rope around the middle of the Sun, and the other to their biggest ship. Then the ship pulled and pulled.

'Heave-ho! Heave-ho!' cried the sailors.

Up came the Sun, inch by inch. Then SNAP! The rope gave way. The plan had failed.

It was time for morning – except, of course, there can't be a morning without the Sun. Not that the Sun cared. He was still sitting there, blowing bubbles in the sea.

The Moon frowned. 'I suppose I'll have to shine all day now,' she said. 'What a nuisance! But I feel sorry for the people down there. It isn't their fault.' Looking down, she called out, 'Can't the fishermen help?'

'Yes,' cried the people. 'They're making a net right now. They're going to lift the Sun from the water, as if they were catching fish.'

All day long the fishermen worked by moonlight, making a huge net. At last it was finished. It fitted around the Sun perfectly. But when the fishermen lifted the Sun up, he was so heavy that he fell right through the net and into the water again with a splash.

Another day was gone, and the Moon was still shining all by herself. 'There must be a way,' she said. 'Perhaps the soldiers can help.'

The soldiers thought for a while. Then they had an idea.

'Pulling and lifting haven't worked,' they said. 'So we're going to blast the Sun out of the water. It's the only way to get him into the sky again. Let's get the gunpowder!'

The soldiers brought big barrels of gunpowder, and stacked them carefully around the Sun. Then they lit the fuse.

BANG! went the gunpowder.

'Ouch!' cried the Sun. But after all the smoke had cleared, there he was, still sitting in the water. Now, though, he looked very, very sorry for himself.

'I'm tired of being pulled and lifted and blown up,' he said. 'And it's no fun blowing bubbles any more. I want to go home now.'

The people were worried. They had tried everything, and nothing had worked. They couldn't see very well in the moonlight, and they were getting cold. The flowers wouldn't open, and the wheat was beginning to droop.

The Moon was beginning to droop, too. 'Oh, dear,' she sighed wearily. 'I'm so tired, it wouldn't surprise me if *I* fell into the sea, too.' That made the people even more worried.

But there was one small creature who wasn't worried. That was Jonathan Fin, the fish.

Jonathan was so little, and so plain and brown, that no one ever noticed him. So when he said, 'I've got an idea,' everyone was surprised.

'What?' the people cried. '*You?*'

'Yes, me,' said Jonathan. 'I'd like to try.'

The people agreed to let him try. After all, things couldn't get much worse.

Away swam Jonathan, out to sea. There was the Sun, sitting sadly in the water.

'Oh, dear,' he was saying. 'I want to go home. I really want to go home.'

Jonathan swam towards the Sun but the Sun didn't see him, for the little fish was swimming deep in the water. Backwards and forwards he swam. And as he swam, he tickled the Sun's belly with his long fins.

'Ho! Ho!' giggled the Sun. 'Ha! Ha! Hee! Hee!'

Jonathan kept tickling.

'HO! HO!' roared the Sun. 'HA! HA! HEE! HEE! Stop! I can't stand it!'

Then WHOOSH! With a tremendous leap, he sprang right back into the sky!

The whole world turned sunny again, and the Moon at last sank into her bed – but not before she had said 'Thank you' to the little fish. The people all said 'Thank you' to Jonathan, too.

But Jonathan said nothing – not because he was shy, but because something remarkable had happened to him. His scales had turned bright orange from being so close to the Sun!

'Why, I'm a goldfish now!' he cried excitedly. And indeed he was.

From then on, everyone noticed him. The people put him in a big glass bowl, where he swam about very happily.

As for the Sun, he was so glad to be home and so delighted at being tickled that he hasn't stopped laughing since.

No wonder he looks so cheerful up there in the sky!

Valerie J Appleby

Mr and Mrs Vinegar

Mr and Mrs Vinegar lived in a vinegar bottle that had a wooden door. Mrs Vinegar was a very good housekeeper, and she kept the bottle clean and shining. But one morning, as she was sweeping, she accidentally hit the broom handle against the wall. The vinegar bottle was smashed to bits.

Mrs Vinegar ran to tell her husband what had happened. 'We're ruined!' she cried. 'Where will we live now?'

'Don't worry, dear,' said Mr Vinegar. 'The important thing is that you're not hurt. We can go into the world now, to seek our fortune.'

So Mr and Mrs Vinegar set out. Their wooden door was still in one piece, so they took it with them.

All day they tramped through the countryside, and by nightfall they were exhausted. They had come to a forest, and they decided to stop and rest there.

'I'll climb up into one of the trees,' said Mr Vinegar to his wife, 'and I'll set our door down among the branches. Then you climb up after me. The door will be a bed for us, and we'll be able to sleep quite safely and comfortably.'

Mr and Mrs Vinegar settled down to sleep in the treetop. But in the night, they were awakened by the sound of voices below them.

'Here's your share, Dingo – ten gold pieces,' said a gruff voice. 'Biff, you only stood lookout, so you get five gold pieces.'

'Oh, my goodness,' whispered Mrs Vinegar. 'They're robbers!'

She and her husband were so frightened that they began to tremble. They shivered and quaked and quivered until the door began to shake, too. Before they knew it, they went crashing to the ground.

The robbers were so startled that they fled in terror. They didn't even stop to take their sack of money.

'Look!' said Mr Vinegar, when they'd gone. 'There are forty gold pieces here!'

'We can buy a cow with that money,' said his wife. 'The cow will give us milk, and we can make butter and cheese to sell.'

'Our fortune is made!' cried Mr Vinegar.

Early the next morning, Mr Vinegar set out to buy a cow. Mrs Vinegar stayed behind with the wooden door.

Mr Vinegar came to a town with a busy marketplace. There he met a farmer with a fat red cow. 'What a handsome cow!' said Mr Vinegar.

'Yes,' said the farmer. 'And she gives plenty of good, sweet milk.'

'I'll give you forty gold pieces for her,' said Mr Vinegar.

Now, forty gold pieces was far too much to pay for one cow. But the farmer didn't want to tell Mr Vinegar that. He just said, 'That's a fine bargain!' and gave Mr Vinegar the cow.

Feeling very pleased with himself, Mr Vinegar led the cow through the marketplace. All at once he heard a lovely sound. It was a man playing the bagpipes. A crowd had gathered around the man, and the people were all smiling and clapping their hands and dancing.

When the man finished playing, Mr Vinegar went to talk to him. 'It must be a great joy to spend your days bringing such happiness to people,' he said. 'I would give anything to make my living that way. Would you trade your bagpipes for this cow?'

The man looked at the cow. 'She's a fine-looking animal,' he said. 'It seems to be a fair exchange.' He gave the bagpipes to Mr Vinegar.

But Mr Vinegar didn't know how to play the bagpipes. Though he blew and squeezed with all his might, the only sound he could make was a wheezing, screeching moan. People covered their ears and ran away when they heard it.

Finally Mr Vinegar had to leave the marketplace. He walked sadly back towards the forest.

It was a chilly day, and before long Mr Vinegar's hands began to ache with the cold. Just then, a man came along wearing a pair of thick, woolly gloves.

'Those gloves look nice and warm,' said Mr Vinegar. 'If I could have them, I'd be the happiest man in the world.'

'I'd be glad to give them to you,' said the man, 'if you have something to offer in exchange.'

'Will you take these bagpipes?' asked Mr Vinegar.

'All right,' the man said.

Mr Vinegar put on the gloves and went happily on his way. Soon, however, his legs grew tired. Just as he was about to stop and rest, a man came along with a stout walking stick.

'That stick is exactly what I need,' said Mr Vinegar. 'If I could have it, I'd be the happiest man in the world.'

'I wouldn't mind trading it for those nice thick gloves you're wearing,' said the man.

'Done!' said Mr Vinegar. He exchanged the gloves for the stick, and went on his way feeling quite content.

He hadn't gone very far when he came to a clump of trees. All along the roadside were sticks just as stout and sturdy as the one he'd traded the gloves for. Mr Vinegar realised he hadn't made such a good exchange, after all. In fact, he began to feel very foolish.

High above Mr Vinegar, a raven flew among the branches. 'Haw! Haw! Haw!' it called. Mr Vinegar was sure the bird was laughing at him.

'You impudent creature!' he shouted. 'I'll teach you to laugh at me!' And he threw the walking stick at the bird.

Now Mr Vinegar had nothing – no walking stick, no gloves, no bagpipes, no cow, and no money. 'Oh, what have I done?' he moaned. Gloomily, he made his way back to where his wife was waiting.

'Well, at least we still have our wooden door,' said Mrs Vinegar, when her husband came back empty-handed. 'We're no worse off than when we set out.'

The next morning they started on their travels again. Luckily, they found another vinegar bottle someone had thrown out, and they set up house again. And this time, Mrs Vinegar was very, *very* careful when she did her sweeping!

The wolf and the fox

A wolf and a fox once shared a home in the forest. The wolf was very bossy, and because he was stronger than the fox, the fox had to do everything the wolf told him to.

One day the wolf said, 'I'm hungry, Foxy. Get me something to eat, or I'll eat *you*.'

The fox had no choice but to obey. 'Today's the day the farmer's wife bakes her bread,' he said. 'There must be some loaves in the oven right now. I'll get you one.' And he ran off.

Soon he was back with a fresh, warm loaf of bread. The wolf gobbled it up.

'That was delicious,' said the wolf. 'But what about the other loaves?'

'I only took one,' said the fox.

'Well, I'm going to get some more,' said the wolf. 'Wait for me – I'll be back soon.'

The wolf ran to the farmhouse and sneaked into the kitchen. 'Now I'll have a feast!' he said to himself. But he was very clumsy, and he made such a racket trying to open the oven door that the farmer's wife heard him and came after him with her broom.

A little while later the wolf came stumbling home. 'I was caught,' he told the fox. 'The farmer's wife gave me a terrible beating.'

'Perhaps you shouldn't have been so greedy,' said the fox.

The next day the wolf said again, 'I'm hungry, Foxy. Get me something to eat, or I'll eat *you*.'

'All right,' sighed the fox. 'The farmer and his wife are having roast chicken for dinner. I'll see if I can get you some.'

Soon the fox came back with a juicy roast chicken. The wolf grabbed it and gobbled it up. 'That was very tasty,' he said, licking his lips, 'but it was only an appetiser. Isn't there any more?'

'There were three chickens in the kitchen,' said the fox, 'but I only took one.'

'Well, I'm going to get the rest,' said the wolf. 'Wait for me – I'll be back soon.'

Once again the wolf sneaked into the farmhouse kitchen. There on the table were two plump roast chickens on a platter. The wolf's mouth watered at the sight. He reached up to get the chickens, but he was in such a hurry that he knocked the platter off the table, and it fell to the floor with a crash. The farmer, who was working in the garden right outside, came rushing in with his rake.

Some time later, the wolf came limping home. His tail was bent and he had a bump on his head. 'Look what happened to me!' he said to the fox. 'The farmer beat me to a pulp!'

'Maybe you shouldn't have been so greedy,' said the fox.

But the next day the wolf was hungry again. 'Get me something to eat, Foxy,' he said, 'or I'll eat *you*.'

This time, the fox had a plan. 'The farmer and his wife have a big barrel of smoked ham in their cellar,' he told the wolf. 'I could go and get you some, but if you came with me, we could get twice as much.'

'Let's go!' said the wolf.

The fox led the way to the farmer's cellar. All the doors were locked, so they had to go in through a tiny little window.

There was plenty of ham in the barrel, and the fox and the wolf both helped themselves. But while the fox ate just enough and no more, the wolf kept stuffing himself. 'I won't stop until this barrel's empty!' he said.

'If I were you, I wouldn't be so greedy,' said the fox. But the wolf paid no attention to him. He just kept eating.

All at once they heard footsteps. The farmer was coming!

The fox quickly slipped through the tiny window and got out safely. But the wolf had eaten so much that he was too fat to fit through the window, and he got stuck halfway. The farmer beat him mercilessly, and wouldn't let him go until he promised never to come back to the farm again.

Late that night, when the bruised and battered wolf came hobbling home at last, the fox said to him, 'I told you not to be so greedy, didn't I?'

'Yes, and you were right,' said the wolf. 'That's the last time I'll ever be such a glutton!'

And it was.

The king's lazy soldiers

Most soldiers are very, very neat. Their uniforms are pressed. Their buttons are bright and shiny. Their boots are polished. Soldiers always stand tall, in long straight lines.

Long ago, however, there lived a king who had the sloppiest soldiers anyone had ever seen. They were always late for duty, and they never looked right. Some had their uniforms on inside-out. Some had buttons missing. Some had their boots on the wrong feet. One soldier even lost his trousers once!

They were a mess. And it was all because they couldn't get up in the morning. Even the soldier who blew the bugle to wake the others couldn't get up on time.

'You're a perfect disgrace!' shouted the king one morning. 'Something must be done. Tomorrow I will wake you all up with a bang!'

But the soldiers didn't want to wake up early. So that night, before they went to bed, they worked out a plan of their own.

The next morning at dawn, the king crept out to the biggest cannon on the palace grounds – and fired it. There was an enormous BANG! The whole palace shook for five minutes.

The king waited and waited, but not one soldier appeared. They were still fast asleep.

The soldiers had been very clever. Before they'd gone to sleep, they had put pillows over their ears. They hadn't heard a thing.

'Tomorrow *I'll* wake them up,' promised the queen. 'I know something that will make their ears ring!'

But that night, before they went to bed, the soldiers worked out another plan.

Early the next morning, the queen had the big bell from the palace tower placed just outside the soldiers' room. She pulled the rope as hard as she could. The ringing was heard for miles around.

The queen waited and waited, but not one soldier appeared. They were still fast asleep.

This time, the clever soldiers had stuffed cotton in their ears!

'Now it's my turn to try,' said the prince. 'Just wait until tomorrow morning. They'll be out of bed in a flash!'

The soldiers were puzzled. What could the prince be up to?

Early the next morning, the prince crept into the soldiers' room. Hidden behind his back was a long curly feather.

All at once the prince began to tickle the soldiers' bare feet. Soon the soldiers were screaming with laughter and falling out of bed.

The prince ran out, shouting, 'They're up! They're awake! They're all out of bed!' The king and queen were thrilled.

Everyone waited, but not one soldier appeared. They were fast asleep again. The laughing and giggling had made them all so tired that they had gone back to bed.

Now the princess, who had said nothing till now, just smiled to herself. She had thought of a very special plan.

Very early the next morning, the princess tiptoed into the palace kitchen and whispered something to the cook. Soon everyone in the kitchen was busy boiling, baking, slicing and toasting.

The soldiers were fast asleep, of course. But in a little while wonderful smells began to drift through their door, across their beds, and under their noses. Smells of crisp buttery toast and fluffy scrambled eggs. Smells of sweet orange juice and creamy hot cocoa. Smells of oatmeal with cinnamon and hot muffins with honey.

'Mmmmmm, what lovely smells,' murmured one soldier.

'We're having breakfast in bed!' said another soldier happily.

'Oh, no, you're not!' snapped the princess, coming into the room. 'When you're up and dressed and have reported for duty, *then* you can have breakfast – not before.'

In no time at all, the men had put on their uniforms and boots and hats. The princess checked to make sure they were all neat and clean. At last they were ready.

What a wonderful sight they made as they marched into the palace yard: every boot was polished, every button was shining, every uniform was pressed. The soldiers stood tall and proud, and marched in a long straight line.

The king and queen were speechless.

The princess kept her promise, and they all had breakfast together. Everything tasted just as wonderful as it smelled. 'I think we'll do this every morning,' the soldiers decided.

The princess just smiled and munched her toast.

Ann McKie

The magpie's nest

Birds are clever creatures. Think of all the things they know how to do: they know how to fly, and how to sing, and how to lay eggs and hatch them, and how to build nests.

But they haven't always known how to do these things. They had to take lessons. Not every bird went to every lesson, of course. The penguin and the ostrich, for instance, missed their flying lessons. The crow and the chicken never learned to sing. And on the day when the other birds were learning nest-building, the magpie was far away, collecting bright-coloured berries and bits of shiny stones and shells.

The next day, when the magpie returned home, she had lots of pretty things. But she had nowhere to keep them.

'What you need is a nest,' said the sparrow. 'We learned how to build nests yesterday.'

'Oh, really?' said the magpie. She was very proud, so she didn't want to appear too interested.

'Yes,' said the robin. 'We'll show you how, if you like.'

'Oh, all right,' said the magpie. 'But I'm sure I know it all already.'

The pigeon picked up a twig. 'First you take a little stick like this,' she said, 'and you set it down this way.' She put the twig on a branch.

'Oh, yes,' said the magpie, yawning. 'I know that already.'

'Then,' said the blackbird, 'you get another twig, and put it down this way.' She laid the second twig on the first so that it balanced perfectly.

'Oh, I know that already,' said the magpie, looking round, bored.

The thrush and the starling followed, showing her how to place the twigs one on top of the other. The magpie paid no attention. She just tossed her head and said, 'Oh, I know that already.'

The swallow and the wren showed her how to make the nest neat and strong with mud, and how to make it warm by lining it with feathers. The magpie gave a little sniff. 'Yes,' she said. 'I know that already.'

Finally the other birds grew tired of the magpie's conceited manner. 'All right, Mrs Know-It-All Magpie,' they said. 'Since you know so much, you can finish the nest yourself!' And they all flew off, leaving the magpie with a half-made nest.

Of course, the magpie had no idea how to finish the nest. And she still doesn't. To this day, a messy, half-finished bundle of sticks is the only kind of nest a magpie can make.

Foolish Jack

Once there was a boy named Jack who never thought for himself. He always did what he was told, but he couldn't seem to work out anything on his own. If his mother told him to feed the dog, she had to tell him *what* to feed the dog – or he might put a cabbage or an onion in poor Fido's bowl. If she asked him to hang the washing out to dry, she had to remind him to hang it on the clothesline. Otherwise, she might find socks and towels and bedsheets flapping from the trees and the fence. The neighbours all laughed at Jack, and everyone called him 'Foolish Jack'.

One day Jack's mother said to him, 'Perhaps if you went out to work you'd learn not to be so foolish. Farmer Field needs help with his planting. Why don't you see if you can work for him?'

So, early on Monday morning, Jack set off for the farm. He was determined to listen carefully to what Farmer Field told him, and to do everything right.

Jack was a good worker, and at the end of the day Farmer Field said to him, 'You have been a big help to me. Please come back tomorrow. In the meantime, here's a coin for your day's wages.'

Jack thanked the farmer and wrapped the coin up in his handkerchief. But on the way home, he dropped the handkerchief and lost the coin.

'Foolish Jack!' said his mother. 'You should have put the coin in your pocket.'

'Next time I will,' Jack promised.

On Tuesday Jack worked hard and again Farmer Field was pleased with him. This time he gave Jack a pitcher of fresh milk to take home.

Jack didn't want to lose the milk in the same way as he had lost the coin. Remembering what his mother had told him, he put the pitcher in his pocket. But as soon as he took one step, the pitcher turned over and all the milk spilled out.

'Foolish Jack!' said his mother when he got home. 'You should have carried the pitcher on your head.'

'Next time I will,' Jack said.

On Wednesday Farmer Field gave Jack half a dozen eggs. Jack remembered what his mother had said, and he put the eggs on top of his head. Of course, they all rolled off and splattered on the ground.

'Foolish Jack!' said his mother. 'You should have carried the eggs in your hands.'

'Next time I will, Mother,' said Jack.

On Thursday Farmer Field gave Jack a wriggly little piglet. Jack tried to carry it home in his hands, but it was so wriggly that it wriggled free and ran away.

'Foolish Jack!' said his mother. 'You should have tied a string round its neck and led it home.'

'Next time I will,' Jack said.

On Friday Farmer Field gave Jack a big roast beef to take home. Jack carefully tied a string round it so he could lead it home. Naturally, by the time he got home there was nothing left – it had all been eaten by dogs along the way!

'Foolish Jack!' said his mother. 'Why didn't you carry the roast on your shoulder?'

'Next time I will,' said Jack.

Saturday was Jack's last day at the farm. All the planting was done, and Farmer Field was very grateful for Jack's help. So he gave Jack something special to take home – a brown and white spotted calf.

Jack struggled and strained and lifted, and finally he managed to get the calf onto his shoulder. Huffing and puffing, he started for home.

Jack didn't know it, but Farmer Field's daughter Annie had been watching him from her window all week. When she'd seen him with milk spilling out of his pocket, her eyes had opened wide. When she'd seen him trying to balance eggs on his head, her eyes had twinkled. When she'd seen him leading a roast beef on a string, she had smiled. Now, when she saw him with a gangly calf slung over his shoulder and his own legs wobbling like jelly, she burst out laughing and laughed as if she would never stop.

'Jack!' she called, when she could finally catch her breath. 'Jack, come here.'

Jack lurched and stumbled to the window. 'Yes?' he said, blushing. He suddenly felt shy, for Annie was very pretty.

'I think you are the funniest person I have ever seen,' said Annie. 'Most of the time I feel gloomy and sad, but not when I see you. You make me feel happy, Jack!'

For the first time in his life, Jack had a thought of his own. He put down the calf and said, 'If we got married, you could be happy all the time!'

'What a good idea!' said Annie.

So Jack and Annie were married. From then on, Annie *was* happy all the time, and Jack began to think for himself at last – and he was never called 'Foolish Jack' again.

The gifts of the little folk

Once, a very long time ago, a tailor and a carpenter were travelling through the countryside together. One evening, after the sun had set, they heard music in the distance. It sounded strange, but it was so pleasant that they forgot how tired they were and hurried to find out where it was coming from.

They walked on and on, and at last they came to a hill. By then the moon had risen, and they could see a crowd of tiny men and women, holding hands and dancing merrily in a ring. They sang as they danced, and their sweet, high-pitched singing was the music the travellers had heard. In the middle of the circle sat an old man with a long grey beard. He was slightly bigger than the others, and he wore a splendid coat of many colours.

The travellers stood watching the dance in amazement. When the old man saw them, he beckoned to them to enter the circle, and the little folk graciously made an opening for them. The carpenter boldly stepped right in. The tailor was a little uneasy and hung back at first, but when he saw how happy and cheerful they all were, he grew brave and followed.

The circle closed, and the little folk went on singing and dancing Then the old man took a knife from his belt and looked at the travellers. They were frightened, but there was no time to escape. Quick as a flash, the old man grabbed them and cut off all their hair.

As soon as the old man had finished, he gave them each a warm, friendly pat on the back, as if to thank them and say they had done well. Then he pointed to a pile of coal that lay off to one side, and motioned to them to take some. They couldn't imagine what they would do with the coal, but they each put some in their pockets and thanked the old man.

Off in the distance, a clock struck twelve. Instantly the singing and dancing stopped, the little folk vanished, and the hill stood deserted in the moonlight.

The two travellers made their way to the nearest town, where they found an inn. They were so tired that they lay down to sleep without even taking off their coats.

By morning their coats felt so heavy that the men awoke very early. When they reached into their pockets, they couldn't believe what they found: not coal, but pure gold! And when they looked at one another, they saw that their hair had grown back, as thick as before.

Both men were now rich, but the carpenter, who was greedy, had put more coal in his pockets and was twice as rich as the tailor. Because greedy people always want more, he said they should go back to the little folk for more treasure.

The tailor shook his head. 'This is enough for me,' he said. 'Now I can set myself up as a master tailor and marry my sweetheart. I'll be a happy man.'

But the carpenter kept pestering him, and at last the tailor agreed. 'But I'll wait for you here,' he said. 'I am content with what I have, so you will have to go to the hill alone.'

That evening the carpenter walked back to the hill. Again he found the little folk singing and dancing in a circle. Again the little old man cut off his hair and invited him to take some coal. The carpenter quickly grabbed as much as he could, and he left with his pockets bulging.

He went back to the inn overjoyed, and lay down without taking off his coat. 'No matter how much that gold weighs,' he said to himself, 'I'll bear it gladly.' He fell asleep thinking happy thoughts of what he would do with his great riches.

The moment his eyes opened in the morning, the carpenter jumped up to look in his pockets. Much to his surprise, all he could find was black, dusty coal. He reached in again and again, but nothing changed except that his hands got dirtier and dirtier.

'Well, at least I still have the gold I took the night before,' he thought, and went to get it. To his horror, all the gold had been turned back to coal! He clapped his filthy hand to his forehead, and realised that his head was still as bald as an egg. To make things worse, when he went to wash his hands, the coal dust wouldn't come off, no matter how hard he scrubbed.

The carpenter knew then that he had been punished for his greed, and he sat down and began to weep. His sobs woke the tailor, who did his best to comfort his unhappy friend. 'You've been with me through all my travels,' said the tailor. 'I will be glad to share my treasure with you.'

The tailor kept his word, but the poor carpenter had to live with his dirty hands for the rest of his days, and wear a cap to keep his bald head warm.

The princess and the salt

Once upon a time, there was a king who had three daughters. One of them would be queen someday, and the king had to decide which of them it should be. It was a difficult decision, for all the princesses were clever and good, and he loved them all dearly.

The king thought and thought, and at last he had an idea. He asked each of his daughters to bring him a gift. 'The one who brings me the most precious gift will be queen,' he said.

The eldest daughter brought the king a coat made of silver silk and trimmed with rubies. The king was pleased.

The second daughter brought him a golden bird with a voice like crystal bells. The king was very pleased.

The third daughter brought a small covered dish.

'There must be something very precious in this dish,' thought the king as he lifted the lid. But when he saw what it was, he was furious.

'This is nothing but plain, common salt!' he shouted. 'What sort of gift is this? I have never seen such disrespect in my life!'

'But, Father – ' said the princess, trying to explain.

'You are no longer a daughter of mine,' said the king, interrupting her. 'Leave the palace at once, and never come back!'

Filled with grief and despair, the princess left. She had nowhere to go, and she wandered the countryside sadly for many weeks.

At last, far from the palace, she came to an inn. The innkeeper didn't know that she was a princess, but he felt sorry for her and said she could stay if she would work in the kitchen.

The princess became the cook's helper. The cook was kind and taught the princess everything she knew, and the princess was quick to learn. Before long she was even better than the cook. People began coming from miles around to taste the tempting dishes she made.

As time went by, people all over the kingdom heard about the cook who could turn a simple meal into a mouth-watering feast. Eventually, the king himself heard about her.

'She must come to work in the palace kitchen,' he said.

So the princess went to the palace to cook for her own father. No one, least of all the king, had any idea who she really was.

The time came when the king's eldest daughter was to be married. A huge wedding banquet was planned, and important guests from many lands were invited. In the kitchen the princess worked very hard to get everything ready on time.

On the day of the wedding the king and his guests sat down in the banqueting hall. Everyone knew about the king's wonderful cook, and they were looking forward to a splendid meal.

Servants marched in carrying trays of the most delicious-looking food anyone had ever seen. The king glowed with pride. When everyone had been served, he lifted his fork to take the first bite. The guests all waited and watched for the sign that they could begin eating, too.

To everyone's amazement, the king made a horrible face and spat out the food. He tasted something else, and the same thing happened. He tried one dish after another, and with each mouthful he only scowled harder. His guests couldn't understand what was happening.

At last, in a terrifying voice, the king roared, 'GET ME THE COOK!'

The cook was brought in. She stood before the king with her head bowed.

'You have cooked the food without salt!' the king bellowed. 'How dare you forget something so important?'

'I did not forget,' said the cook.

'WHAT?' cried the king. 'Then you have deliberately shamed me before my guests! You will go to prison for this! Have you anything to say before you are taken away?'

'I do,' said the princess. 'A long time ago, you banished your daughter – because she gave you a gift of common salt.'

'Yes,' said the king quietly. 'I remember that awful day. Now I understand how precious her gift was – and what a fool I was. But how can you possibly know about that?'

The princess looked up. When the king saw her face, he sprang to his feet.

'My daughter!' he cried. 'It's you! Welcome home, my child!' Tears of joy filled his eyes as he took her in his arms.

And so the day ended more happily than anyone had expected, and the princess once again took her rightful place in the palace.

The three wishes

A poor woodcutter once lived with his wife in a tiny cottage at the edge of a forest. They worked hard, and they struggled to get by. Though they dreamed of having a big house and fine clothes, they never had enough money for more than the bare necessities.

One evening, as the woodcutter was going home, a white rabbit ran across his path. It seemed very frightened, and in a moment the woodcutter saw why – a big red fox was chasing it. The woodcutter picked up a stick and threw it, frightening the fox away.

The white rabbit hopped back to the woodcutter. To the woodcutter's amazement, it began to speak.

'Thank you for saving me from the fox,' it said. 'In return, I would like to do something for you. Because you have helped me, I will give you three wishes. You may wish for anything you want. But think carefully and choose your wishes wisely, for you may have only three!' Then the rabbit hopped away into the forest.

Overjoyed, the woodcutter ran home. 'You'll never believe what happened!' he told his wife. 'I met a magic rabbit in the woods, and it gave me three wishes. We can have anything now, anything we want!'

'We can wish for a new house,' said his wife.

'Even a palace!' said the woodcutter.

'We can wish for gold and silver,' said his wife.

'Or emeralds and rubies!' said the woodcutter.

'Oh, I can't think!' said his wife. 'Let's eat supper first. We'll be able to make a better decision when our bellies are full.'

She took a big pot off the stove and put it on the table. Her husband lifted the lid and looked inside.

'Not boiled potatoes *again!*' he groaned. 'I'm so tired of potatoes! That's all we ever have. I wish we had a nice juicy sausage to eat with them.'

Instantly, a big fat sausage appeared on the table.

'Look what you've done!' cried his wife. 'You've wasted one of our precious wishes on a silly sausage! Now we only have two wishes left.'

'That's all right,' said her husband. 'Two wishes can still get us plenty of good things.'

'But three could have given us more,' said his wife. 'How could you be such a ninny? Only a fool would wish for a sausage. Oh, what a sausage-head I married!' And she went on and on, complaining and calling her husband names.

At last the woodcutter had had enough. 'Be quiet!' he shouted. 'I'm sick of your complaints, and I'm sick of hearing about that sausage! I wish that sausage was stuck on your nose!'

As soon as the words were out of his mouth, the sausage went right onto the end of his wife's nose.

'Oh, no!' she cried. 'Look what you've done now!'

She tugged and pulled at the sausage, but it would not come off. She shouted and cried and pulled harder, but the sausage was stuck fast. Her husband pulled, too, with all his might, but nothing would move that sausage.

'Never mind,' said the woodcutter at last. 'We have one wish left. Think of all the wonderful things we can still wish for.'

'But what good would anything be?' wailed his wife. 'Even if we lived in a castle and had all the money in the world, where could I go with a sausage stuck to my nose? Everyone would laugh at me! There's only one thing to do – we have to wish the sausage off again.'

'But then we'd be right back where we started,' said the woodcutter.

'I don't care,' said his wife. 'I wish this sausage was gone!'

Quick as a wink, the sausage disappeared.

And the woodcutter and his wife had no wishes left, and they were just as poor as ever. They didn't even have the nice juicy sausage to eat with their potatoes.

The queen bee

Once there were three brothers named Ronald, Donald, and Jasper, who decided to go off in search of adventure. They packed their packs and climbed on their horses, and they set out.

As they were riding through the woods, the brothers saw an ant hill on the path in front of them. Ronald and Donald were about to let their horses gallop over it and trample it, but Jasper stopped them.

'Why not ride round it?' he said. 'There's no need to harm the ants.' So they rode round the ant hill, and the ants were saved.

A little farther on they came to a lake. Some ducks swam by, close to the shore.

Ronald and Donald jumped off their horses and began throwing stones at the ducks. 'Why are you doing that?' cried Jasper.

'If we can kill one of those ducks,' said Donald, 'we can roast it and have a tasty meal!'

'But we have plenty of food in our packs,' said Jasper. 'There's no need to hurt the ducks.'

So Ronald and Donald stopped throwing stones, and the ducks were saved.

The three brothers rode on, and in a little while they came to a tree with a beehive in it. There was so much honey in the hive that it dripped and ran down the tree trunk.

'That looks delicious!' said Ronald. 'If we make a fire at the bottom of the tree, the smoke will smother the bees and we can get all that honey for ourselves!'

'You're right,' said Donald, and he began looking in his pack for matches.

'It would be cruel to harm the bees,' said Jasper. 'Let's leave them in peace.'

So the three brothers rode on, and the bees were saved.

At last the brothers came to a castle. The gates were open, so they rode into the courtyard and went inside.

The castle was still and quiet. Nothing stirred. There were stone statues everywhere, but the brothers didn't see a sign of another person. They were about to turn round and leave, when they passed a room where a tiny dwarf sat at a table.

'Come in,' said the dwarf. 'Have you come to try and break the spell?'

'What spell?' asked the brothers.

'Many years ago,' said the dwarf, 'this castle was put under a magic spell, and the king and his family have been asleep ever since. Only when the spell is broken will they wake up again.'

'What do we have to do?' asked the brothers.

'There are three tasks,' said the dwarf, 'and you must complete them all. If you fail in any one of them, you will be turned to stone. All those statues you saw are people who have been unsuccessful. Do you want to try?'

'Yes,' said all three brothers at once.

'The first task,' said the dwarf, 'is to find the princesses' pearls. One day the king's three daughters were walking in the woods, and their pearl necklaces broke. Now there are a thousand pearls scattered in the forest. One of you must find them all and bring them back to me before sunset. But if you miss even one, you will be turned to stone.'

Early the next morning, Ronald set out to find the pearls. He looked all day, but by sunset he had found only a few hundred, and he was turned to stone.

The next day Donald went out to look. He was as unlucky as his brother, and he too was turned to stone.

Then it was Jasper's turn. He searched and searched, but as sunset drew near, he had found only a few pearls. He was about to give up when he saw a line of a thousand ants marching towards him. They were the ants he had saved a few days before. In no time at all, each ant had found a pearl and given it to Jasper.

'Thank you!' Jasper cried, hurrying back to the dwarf.

When Jasper had given him the pearls, the dwarf said, 'Now you are ready for the second task. A golden key lies at the bottom of a lake near here. You must find it and fish it out.'

Jasper rode to the lake, which was the same one he and his brothers had passed on their travels. As he stood on the shore wondering how to find the key, the ducks he had saved swam up to him. The biggest duck quacked, dived under the water, and came up with the golden key in its bill.

'Thank you!' cried Jasper, and he took the key back to the dwarf.

'You've done well,' said the dwarf. 'Only one task remains.'

'What is it?' asked Jasper.

'Use this key to unlock the room where the princesses are sleeping,' said the dwarf. 'Then you must decide which princess is the youngest, and kiss her. It will not be easy, for all three princesses look alike, and if you kiss the wrong one first, you will be turned to stone instantly. The only thing I can tell you is that the youngest princess was eating honey before she fell asleep. Now go, and good luck!'

Jasper unlocked the door to the princesses' room. There were the three princesses, all fast asleep. They were all beautiful, and they did all look exactly alike. Jasper was about to take a chance and kiss the first one, when suddenly a bee came buzzing into the room. It was the queen bee from the hive Jasper had saved. She buzzed and flitted from one princess to the next, tasting the lips of each one. At last she stopped at the third. Jasper realised that this was the princess with honey on her lips, and he kissed her.

Suddenly the three princesses woke up. In the next room, the king and queen woke up. All over the castle, the people who had been turned to stone came to life. The spell was broken!

Jasper stayed at the castle and married the youngest princess. His brothers stayed, too, and married her sisters. And everyone lived happily ever after.

The farmer and the donkey

One day, a farmer and his son decided to take their donkey to market and sell him. On their way to town, they passed a group of people sitting in the sun and gossiping.

'Look at that!' said one woman, laughing. 'Why are those two trudging along on foot when they have a perfectly good donkey to ride? What fools they must be!' All her friends laughed with her.

'Did you hear that?' said the farmer to his son. 'They think we're fools! Quick, get up on the donkey's back before we meet anyone else.'

They travelled like that for a while, until they passed some old men resting outside an inn.

'It's terrible,' said one old man. 'Young people are so selfish nowadays! There's a strong young boy riding in comfort, while his poor old father has to walk. Why doesn't the boy get down and let his father rest his legs?'

'Did you hear that?' said the farmer. 'Get off and let me ride the donkey, or people will think I haven't raised you properly.'

So the two changed places.

They went along that way until they passed a group of children playing in a field.

'Oh, look!' cried one of the children, pointing at the farmer. 'Look at that lazy man riding the donkey while his son has to run after him. What a mean old man!'

'Did you hear that?' the farmer said. 'Jump up behind me, or people will think I'm not a good father to you.'

So they rode along. They were nearly at the marketplace when they passed a little yard filled with cats, dogs, chickens, rabbits, and goats. A woman who was feeding the animals looked up and saw the farmer and his son both riding on the donkey's back.

'Shame on you!' she shouted at them. 'How can you overload a poor little donkey like that? Where are you going with him, anyway?'

'We're taking him to market, to sell him,' replied the farmer.

'Well, he'll be worn out by the time you get there, if he has to carry two great big fellows like you on his back,' said the woman. 'Another few steps, and you'll have to carry *him*!'

'Maybe she's right,' said the farmer to his son. 'After all, we want the donkey to be in good condition when we get him to market, otherwise no one will buy him. Maybe we *should* carry him.'

The farmer grabbed the donkey's front legs, and his son took the back legs. With a tremendous effort, they hoisted the donkey onto their shoulders. Then, staggering and shaking under the weight, they began to walk the rest of the way to the marketplace.

The donkey, who had never been carried in his life, was very uncomfortable. As the farmer and his son struggled beneath him, he wriggled off their shoulders and ran away. The farmer and his son tried to go after him, but by this time they were so tired that they couldn't run more than a few steps.

'Now we have neither donkey nor money,' said the farmer sadly. 'That's what happens when you let other people tell you what to do!' And he and his son slowly made their way back home.

The princess and the pea

Once upon a time there was a prince who decided that it was time to get married. 'I want to marry a princess,' he told his mother and father, 'but she must be a *real* princess.'

'I don't think we know any real princesses,' said his father. 'We know girls who are as pretty as princesses, and girls who are as rich as princesses. Won't any of those do?'

'No,' said the prince. 'She must be a *real* princess.'

'Then you will have to go out and find her,' said the king.

So the prince set out to find a real princess to marry. He travelled to distant cities and foreign lands. Everywhere he went, he met beautiful young ladies who said that they were princesses. But none of them was quite right.

'I'm sorry,' the prince said to each one, 'but you just don't seem to be a *real* princess.'

After travelling for a year, the prince at last gave up and went home. 'I don't think there are any *real* princesses anywhere,' he told his parents sadly. 'I will just have to remain a bachelor.'

One night, not long after the prince had come home, there was a terrible storm in the kingdom. Fierce winds howled and beat against the castle walls, and rain whipped at the windows. Lightning flashed, and thunder pounded and roared.

In the midst of the storm, there was a knock at the palace door. The king himself went to answer it.

At the door stood a wet, shivering girl. Her fine clothes and long golden hair were soaked and streaming, and water ran through her dainty satin slippers.

'I am a princess,' she told the king. 'A *real* princess. May I come in?'

'Of course!' said the king.

He sent his servants to get towels and dry clothes for the girl. Then the king called his wife and son.

'A girl has arrived, and she says she is a *real* princess,' he told them.

The prince's heart leapt with joy. But then he remembered all the other girls who had said that *they* were real princesses, and he grew sad again. 'How can we be sure she is telling the truth?' he asked.

'Leave that to me,' said his mother, and she went to prepare the royal guest room.

First the queen took all the sheets and blankets off the bed. Then she put a tiny pea under the mattress. On top of the mattress she put another mattress, and then another and another, until there were twenty mattresses piled on the bed. Then, on top of the twenty mattresses, she put twenty soft and fluffy feather quilts. 'That should do it,' she said to herself at last.

The king and queen showed the princess to her room. The princess needed a tall ladder to climb into bed.

In the morning, the queen came to see the princess. 'How did you sleep, my dear?' she asked her.

'Terribly!' said the princess. 'I tossed and turned all night, and now I'm black and blue all over. I don't know what was in that bed, but it felt as if I was sleeping on rocks!'

Then the queen knew that the girl had indeed been telling the truth. Only a *real* princess could have skin so tender that she would feel a tiny pea through twenty mattresses and twenty feather quilts.

'She is your true bride,' she told her son.

The prince and the princess were married, and there were joyous celebrations throughout the kingdom. The pea was placed on a velvet cushion and displayed in the royal museum, where it sits to this very day – that is, unless someone has stolen it!

Hans Christian Andersen

The elves and the shoemaker

Once there was a poor shoemaker who kept getting poorer and poorer. At last he and his wife had nothing to eat but stale bread, and all he had left in his shop was enough leather to make one pair of shoes.

The shoemaker cut out the leather and left it on his workbench. 'I'm too tired to do any more work tonight,' he sighed. 'I'll finish the shoes in the morning.'

The next morning, when he went to his workbench, the shoemaker couldn't believe his eyes. There, right where he had left the leather, was a beautiful pair of shoes, all finished.

He picked up the shoes and looked at them. They were perfectly made. Not a stitch was out of place.

'I may as well put these in the window,' he thought.

Soon a well dressed man came into the shop. 'I need a new pair of shoes,' he said. 'May I see the ones in your window?'

'These are perfect!' said the man, when he had tried them on. 'They are the most beautifully made shoes I have ever seen. You deserve a good price for such excellent work.' And he gave the shoemaker five pieces of silver.

With the money, the shoemaker was able to buy some food for himself and his wife, and enough leather for two more pairs of shoes. As before, he cut out the leather and left it on his workbench, so that he could finish making the shoes in the morning.

When he went to his workbench the next day, he found a surprise again. Now there were two pairs of fine shoes waiting for him.

The shoemaker put the shoes in the window, and it was not long before some customers came in and asked to try them on. The customers were pleased with the shoes, and paid the shoemaker well for them.

Now the shoemaker had enough money to buy leather for four pairs of shoes. He cut out the leather and left it, and the next morning found four brand-new pairs of shoes on his workbench.

And so it went on, day after day. The shoemaker would cut out the leather and leave it on his workbench each night, and each morning he would find handsome new shoes waiting for him. Before long he and his wife were rich.

One evening, just before Christmas, the shoemaker and his wife were eating dinner. 'We have been very lucky,' the shoemaker's wife said. 'A few months ago we had nothing but stale bread. Now we eat like kings. We should try to find out who has been helping us, so that we can repay their kindness.'

'You're right,' said the shoemaker. 'Let's stay up tonight, and watch. Maybe we can see who has been doing these good deeds for us.'

That night the shoemaker and his wife hid behind a cupboard in a corner of the shop, and waited.

At midnight the shop door opened, and two tiny elves dressed in rags came running in. They went straight to the shoemaker's workbench, sat down, and began working on the leather he had left there. They sewed and hammered so swiftly and skilfully that the shoemaker could only stare in amazement.

The elves worked without stopping until all the shoes were finished. Then, just before dawn, they left.

The shoemaker's wife turned to him. 'Those little elves have made us rich,' she said. 'We must thank them somehow.'

'Yes,' said the shoemaker. 'But how?'

'Did you see how thin and tattered their clothes were?' said his wife. 'And though they make fine shoes for you, they were barefoot themselves. It's cold outside, and there is snow on the ground. Why don't we make them some warm clothes and boots, so they can keep cosy this winter?'

The elves' clothes were finished by the next evening, and the shoemaker and his wife set everything out on the workbench. Once again they hid and waited for the little men.

At the stroke of midnight the door opened, and the elves bounded in, ready for work. At first they were confused to see tiny clothes instead of cut-out leather on the bench. Then they realised that the clothes were for them.

Joyfully, they put the things on. When they saw their reflections in the shop window, they were so delighted that they sang:

'See what handsome boys we are!
We will work on shoes no more.'

They skipped and danced round the room, over chairs and benches, and out of the door.

The elves never came back, but the shoemaker and his wife never forgot them, and they lived in happiness for the rest of their lives.

The gold ring

Once upon a time, a servant girl named Katrina was out on an errand for her master, when she lost her way in the forest.

As night fell, Katrina grew frightened. 'What can I do?' she thought. 'I'll never find my way out of this forest. I'm sure to starve!' She sat down under a tree and began to cry.

All at once a white dove flew out of the tree and landed gently on her shoulder. The dove had a little gold key in his beak, and he put it in Katrina's hand. 'Do you see that oak tree over there?' the dove said. 'There's a lock on it. If you open it with this key, you'll find plenty of food inside.'

Katrina opened the tree, and found milk and bread and honey. She ate as much as she wanted, and felt quite content. When she had finished, she yawned and said, 'Oh, I'm so tired. If only I could lie down and sleep in my own little bed!'

Just then the dove came back, with another key in his beak. 'Open that pine tree over there,' he said. 'You'll find a bed inside.'

Katrina opened the tree, and sure enough, there was a lovely, soft bed in it. She lay down, and soon she was fast asleep.

In the morning the dove came back, bringing still another key. 'Open that birch tree over there,' he said. 'There are new clothes inside for you.'

When Katrina opened the tree, she could hardly believe her eyes. There were clothes more beautiful than any she had ever seen – dresses of the finest silk and satin, velvet jackets trimmed with gold, slippers of soft pink leather. Katrina quickly chose some things and put them on.

'Now,' said the dove. 'Will you do something for me?'

'Gladly,' said Katrina.

'I will lead you to a hut,' said the dove. 'When you go inside, you will see an old woman sitting on a wooden stool. Don't talk to her, no matter what she says to you. Behind her will be a red door. Open it, and you'll see a table with rings of all kinds spread out on it. Some of them will be magnificent, set with splendid jewels. Leave those alone. Look for a plain gold ring, and bring that one to me as fast as you can.'

Katrina followed the dove to the hut. When she went inside, she saw the old woman.

'Good day, my child,' said the woman. 'How beautiful you look!'

Katrina said nothing. She just walked behind the woman, towards the red door.

'Where are you going?' cried the old woman. 'This is my house! You can't go in there without my permission!' She ran after Katrina and tried to stop her, but Katrina was too quick for her.

When she opened the red door, Katrina saw a table filled with more rings than she could count. They glittered and sparkled invitingly, but she quickly pushed them all aside, looking for the plain gold one. She couldn't find it, and her heart sank.

Then, out of the corner of her eye, Katrina saw the old woman sneaking away with a silver cage in her hand. She ran after her, and grabbed the cage. In it was a tiny bird, who held the plain gold ring in his beak.

With a cry of joy, Katrina took the ring and ran out of the hut. She kept running until she was far away. Then, out of breath, she leaned against a tree to rest.

Suddenly Katrina felt the tree move. Its branches twined around her and became two strong arms. When she turned to look, she saw that the tree had become a handsome young man. He took Katrina in his arms and kissed her tenderly.

'You have saved me,' he said to Katrina. 'A year ago, as I was riding through this forest, that old woman stole my gold ring and cast a spell over me. She turned me into a tree, but for a few hours every day I became a white dove and could fly round. That is how I found you. But not until I got the gold ring back could the spell be broken. You have set me free, Katrina.'

The young man was a king's son, and he took Katrina to his father's palace. There they were married, and lived happily ever after.

The magic kettle

In a village in the mountains of Japan, an old man lived in a tidy little house. He was very proud of his home, and was careful to keep his furniture polished, his walls freshly painted, and his straw mats neat and clean.

One morning, as he was admiring the view from his front window, the old man heard a rumbling noise behind him. He turned round, and in a corner of the room he saw a dusty old iron kettle. He had no idea where it had come from, but he picked it up and looked it over carefully. It seemed to be in good condition, so he took it into the kitchen and cleaned it up.

'What good luck!' he thought. 'My own kettle is getting leaky, and I was going to buy a new one. Now I have one that's as good as new, and I haven't had to pay a thing for it.'

He took his old kettle off the stove, and filled the new one with water and put it in its place. But as soon as the water started to boil, something strange happened. First the handle of the kettle gradually changed shape and became a head. Then the spout grew into a tail. Next, four paws sprang out of the body. In less than a minute the old man found himself watching not a kettle, but a real live furry animal called a tanuki.

The tanuki jumped off the stove and bounded round the room like a frisky kitten. It leapt across the furniture and ran up the walls. The old man was beside himself. 'Stop, you naughty creature!' he cried, running after the little animal. 'You'll dirty my nice clean walls! You'll tear my fresh straw mats! Stop!'

At last the old man managed to catch the tanuki and lock it up in a wooden chest, where it could do no harm. But he knew he couldn't keep it. After much thought, he decided to sell the little animal. He sent for a merchant he knew, called Jimmu.

'I have something very valuable to sell,' the old man told Jimmu. 'It's in here.' And he opened the lid of the wooden chest. To his surprise, there was no tanuki inside. There was only the old kettle.

'Well,' said Jimmu. 'It's an old kettle, but it seems to be in good condition. I'll give you a few coins for it.'

The old man was disappointed. He had hoped to get a lot of money for the tanuki. But when he remembered how much trouble the kettle had caused, he held his tongue. 'All right,' he said, and Jimmu took the kettle away.

When Jimmu got home, he put the kettle down in a corner of his room and forgot all about it.

In the middle of the night, he was awakened by a loud noise. He sat up and looked round, but all he could see was the old kettle sitting in the corner. 'I must have been dreaming,' he thought, and went back to sleep.

A few minutes later, he was awakened again. This time he got out of bed and went to have a closer look. To his amazement, he saw that the kettle had become a tanuki. The animal was busily chasing its own tail. Then it turned a few somersaults, clambered up the walls, and ran across the ceiling, all the while waving its tail playfully.

It was nearly morning before Jimmu could get back to sleep. When he woke up, he jumped out of bed to look for the tanuki. But all he found was the old kettle in the corner.

Jimmu didn't know what to do. 'I need some advice,' he said to himself, and went to talk to his friend next door.

Jimmu's friend wasn't surprised by the story. 'I remember hearing tales of a magic kettle when I was a child,' he said. 'It will bring you luck, Jimmu. Put it on display, and charge admission. It will make you rich. But you must get the tanuki's permission first. Otherwise it might get frightened and run away.'

Jimmu took his friend's advice. After making sure he had the tanuki's permission, he set up a tent and posted signs inviting people to come and see a splendid magic show.

At first only a few people came. Jimmu passed the kettle among them so that they could examine it inside and out. Then he took it back and, setting it on a table, commanded it to become a tanuki. In an instant the handle began to change into a head and the spout into a tail, while four paws appeared at the sides. The people were astonished.

'Dance,' said Jimmu, and the tanuki danced. It moved so gracefully and joyously that the people couldn't keep still themselves. Soon everyone was dancing and having a wonderful time.

After that, more and more people came to Jimmu's tent. In a few weeks the crowds were so big that it was almost impossible to get in.

Jimmu's neighbour had been right – Jimmu soon became rich. Yet he wasn't happy. Deep down inside, he knew that he owed some of his wealth to the old man who had sold him the kettle.

One morning Jimmu took the kettle and went to see the old man. He told him everything that had happened. 'I have no right to keep the kettle any longer,' he said, 'so I have brought it back to you. Inside it you will find a hundred gold pieces. They are my payment to you for allowing me to use the kettle.'

The old man thanked him and shook his hand warmly. 'The kettle is valuable,' he said to Jimmu, 'but I have found something much more valuable – an honest man and a true friend.'

From then on, both men had happiness and good fortune for the rest of their days.

Fifty red nightcaps

Long ago, in a faraway land, there lived a man and a woman named Mr and Mrs Fedora. They earned their living by making caps and selling them at town fairs.

One day, Mrs Fedora decided to make a special cap. She bought the finest wool she could find, and she dyed it bright red, her favourite colour. Then she knitted the wool into a cheerful-looking nightcap, with a long tail and a tassel at the end.

'What a wonderful nightcap!' said her husband, when she showed it to him. 'If you make some more, I'm sure I can get a very good price for them at the next town fair.'

So Mrs Fedora set to work, and soon she had knitted fifty red nightcaps. She put them all in a big sack, and Mr Fedora set off for the fair with them.

It was a very hot day, and it was a long way to the fair. In order to get there, Mr Fedora had to walk through a shady wood. The shade was so cool and tempting that he decided to sit down under a tree and rest for a while.

Before long, Mr Fedora grew sleepy. So he took one of the nightcaps out of the sack, put it on, and settled down for a nap.

High in the tree above him, a big old monkey was watching everything Mr Fedora did. When he saw Mr Fedora put on the beautiful red nightcap, the monkey wanted to do the very same thing.

As soon as Mr Fedora was asleep, the monkey clambered down the tree, took one of the red nightcaps out of the sack, and popped it onto his head. Then he scurried back up the tree, where he sat laughing and chattering and feeling very pleased with himself.

Across the path, another monkey saw him and decided that *he* wanted a red nightcap, too. So the second monkey ran down his tree and got a nightcap out of Mr Fedora's sack. Then a third monkey followed him, and a fourth and a fifth. Soon there were forty nine monkeys, all wearing red nightcaps, sitting in the trees and laughing and calling to one another.

Of course, all the noise woke Mr Fedora. And the first thing he saw was the empty sack beside him.

'Oh, no!' he cried. 'Someone has stolen the red nightcaps! All my wife's hard work, and now I have nothing to sell at the fair! What will I do?' In despair, he pulled his own red nightcap off his head and threw it down on the ground.

High in their trees, the monkeys saw what he had done. And they did the very same thing. One by one, all forty nine monkeys pulled off their red nightcaps and threw them down on the ground.

Surprised and happy, Mr Fedora picked up the caps and put them back in the sack. 'Thank you!' he called to the monkeys.

Then, as the monkeys chattered merrily from the treetops, Mr Fedora made his way to the town fair, where he sold all fifty red nightcaps for a very good price.

MR. AND MRS. VINEGAR
FIFTY RED NIGHTCAPS
THE PRINCES
AND THE SA
THE QUEEN BEE
THE GIFTS OF THE LITTLE FOLK
THE TWELVE DANCING PRINCESSES
THE GOLD RING
MOG AND MAG AND THE BUCKET
THE WOLF AND THE FOX